- OUTDOOR ADVENTURE GUIDES -

CAMPFIRE COOKING

Wild Eats for Outdoor Adventures

by Blake Hoena

Consultant: Gabriel J. Gassman
Outdoor Professional

CAPSTONE PRESS
a capstone imprint

Capstone Captivate is published by Capstone Press, an imprint of Capstone.
1710 Roe Crest Drive
North Mankato, Minnesota 56003
www.capstonepub.com

Cataloging-in-Publication Data is available on the Library of Congress website.
ISBN: 978-1-5435-9033-3 (library binding)
ISBN: 978-1-4966-6617-8 (paperback)
ISBN: 978-1-5435-9034-0 (eBook PDF)

Summary: Provides an introduction to camp cooking, both on a camp stove and over a campfire, including recipes, safety information, and tips and tricks for delicious meals.

Editorial Credits
Editor: Kellie M. Hultgren; Designer: Juliette Peters;
Media Researcher: Morgan Walters; Production Specialist: Katy LaVigne

Photo Credits
Alamy: Clearviewimages RF, 6, Steve Shuey, 15; Capstone Studio/Karon Dubke, 26, 36; Getty Images: Hero Images, 38, 41, 43; iStockphoto: Kris, 10, 19, Lokibaho, bottom right 39, Windzepher, 28, xavierarnau, 5; Juliette Peters, (bark) background 11; Shutterstock: 134lnstudio, (washing) 40, Africa Studio, middle 11, Alexander Hoffmann, (thermometer) 35, aliaksei kruhlenia, (icons) design element, Anna_Pustynnikova, 35, AVN Photo Lab, (fire) design element, Beth Swanson, 24, Brent Hofacker, bottom right Cover, 23, Brett Taylor Photography, 31, Chubykin Arkady, 29, DN1988, (tool) 8, Doriana Smith, top right 45, Dragon Images, 12, Elena Verba, 21, Elena Veselova, 22, Food Travel Stockforlife, (pan) bottom 11, Foxys Forest Manufacture, 7, frantic00, 20, gresei, bottom right 45, Harlan Schwartz, 9, Jay Ondreicka, bottom left Cover, 37, Kirill Z, 34, LianeM, 30, Linda Parton, top right 39, marcin jucha, 17, NSC Photography, 27, Roger Siljander, top 10, Sean Thomforde, bottom 10, Sergey Novikov, 4, shutter_o, (moss) design element, Sorn340 Images, top Cover, 44, Stephanie Creekpaum, 33, Steve Collender, (duct tape) design element throughout, TextureTreasures, (bubbles) 40, Tupungato, 14, VBVVCTND, (khaki) design element throughout, Vereshchagin Dmitry, bottom 8, Victoria Denisova, 13, wideonet, 25, zolotarova viktoriia, 1

Printed and bound in the USA.
PA100

TABLE OF CONTENTS

Words in **bold** are in the glossary.

CHAPTER 1
LET'S EAT!

Come on. Let's eat! There's no need to go hungry while sleeping beneath the stars. It's easy to whip up some tasty grub! You just need to plan and cook more creatively when feeding yourself in the wild.

TYPES OF CAMP COOKING

How do you like to camp? Different people like different kinds of camping. Your style of **roughing it** will help you choose what to eat.

The most common type of camping is car camping. You toss everything into a vehicle and drive to your campsite. You can bring a big camp stove and an ice-filled cooler packed with food.

For hike-in camping, your campsite may be a mile or more away from where you park. You bring only what you can carry in your backpack. That means no big cooler of food and no big camp stove. But you can still eat well if you plan ahead.

COOKING SAFETY

Check to see which ingredients need to stay cool. Most meat, eggs, and dairy products should be kept in a cooler or they will **spoil**. If you're roughing it, leave these foods at home.

MEAL PLAN

To eat well, you need to plan well. Before you head out, make a list of the days you will be camping. For each day, write down the meals you need to prepare. You can eat the same thing for multiple meals. And don't forget snacks!

Once you have your meal plan ready, make a list of all the ingredients you will need to make each meal. Don't forget **condiments**, such as ketchup and mustard!

ROUGHING IT

If you need to keep things lightweight, look for instant (just-add-water) and dried foods. They do not need to be kept cool. And they don't get squished when you stuff them into a backpack.

MAKE A MEAL CHART

Tame your camp cooking stress with a meal chart. Decide what you want to cook each day. Then make copies of your recipes and put them in order, from the first day to the last. You can even decide who will cook each meal.

	FRIDAY	SATURDAY	SUNDAY	MONDAY
BREAKFAST		CHEESY EGGS	BREAKFAST HASH	FLAPJACKS
LUNCH	(DRIVE TO CAMPSITE)	TORTILLA ROLL-UPS	SANDWICHES	(CLEAN UP AND GO)
DINNER	QUESADILLAS	PACKET MEALS	PERSONAL PIZZAS	
SNACKS	S'MORES	GRANOLA	SNACK STACKS	

CHAPTER 2

GEAR UP!

To eat well, each person on your trip needs a set of **utensils**, a plate, and a mug (or cup). You'll also need at least one pot and a frying pan. A metal coffee pot or teakettle is good for boiling water.

You also need a way to cook your food. Old-school campers cook over an open fire. Many campsites have firepits or fire rings for cooking. Some even have a **grate** over the pit to hold food.

Cooking on an open fire takes practice. It's easy to burn your food—or yourself if you aren't careful! A camp stove is easier to use and will soon have you cooking in style.

ROUGHING IT

You do not need to bring a spoon *and* a fork *and* a knife. Camping utensils can do the work of all three!

CAMP STOVES

There are two basic styles of camp stoves. Standard camp stoves have two burners and use a small **propane** tank for fuel. **Canister** stoves are small and lightweight. They have a single burner mounted on top of a small container of fuel. Which one is best for your trip?

CAMP STOVE

Weight: 10 pounds (4.5 kilograms) or more
Burners: 1 or 2
❑ Perfect for car camping
❑ Too bulky to fit in a backpack for hike-in camping

CANISTER STOVE

Weight: Less than 2 pounds (1 kilograms)
Burners: 1
❑ OK for car camping, but too small to cook a lot of food
❑ Perfect for hike-in camping

DISPOSABLE OR REUSABLE?

People often think **disposable** plates, utensils, and cups are best for camping. But using disposables means carrying a lot of extra dishes—one set per person, per meal. A lot of trees and energy go into making paper plates. Plastic utensils and cups also create a lot of trash. **Reusable** items are much friendlier to the environment. And one set of reusable dishes takes up a lot less space in your pack than a bunch of disposable dishes.

disposables

COOKING TIP

A big part of cooking is preparing your ingredients. Make things easier by doing these tasks at home before your camping trip. For example, dice onions and tomatoes and store them in resealable bags in your cooler. You can make hamburger patties ahead of time too.

FISHING AND FORAGING

It can be fun to catch your own food or **forage** for tasty berries. But you can never be sure of finding food in the wild. Bring all the food you need for every meal on your trip. Then, if you reel in a big one or find a blueberry patch, you will have extra treats.

If you plan to look for **edible** plants, be sure to bring along a field guide. Field guides help you identify what plants are safe to eat and which are **toxic**. Never eat anything unless you know exactly what it is.

COOKING SAFETY

Wash fruits and vegetables that have a skin or peel that you eat, such as apples and tomatoes. This removes dirt and other things that could make you ill.

FOOD STORAGE

While camping, your food needs to be stored properly. Do not keep food in your tent! Anything with a scent—including toothpaste and soap—will attract raccoons, squirrels, bears, and other animals. If you are car camping, keep your cooler and other food items in the car at night. If you're roughing it, some campsites have metal lockers to keep your food safe.

You can also hang your food out of animals' reach. Put it in a backpack or bag. Tie one end of a rope to the bag. Tie the other end of the rope to a weight, such as a rock or stick. Then find a tree at least 200 feet (60 meters) from your campsite. Throw the weighted end of the rope up over a limb about 20 feet (6 m) up. Pull the rope until the bag is well above your head. Then tie the rope around the tree's trunk.

CHAPTER 3
BREAKFAST

Breakfast is the most important meal of the day. It gives your body the energy it needs to get moving. If you fill your belly early, you can fill your day with adventure!

CHEESY SCRAMBLED EGGS

High in protein, eggs give your muscles fuel so you can stomp around the woods.

COOKING SAFETY

Before you start cooking, wash your hands with soapy water. Wash your hands again after touching raw meat or eggs. This prevents the spread of germs and **bacteria** that can make people sick.

INGREDIENTS:

- ❑ eggs
- ❑ milk
- ❑ butter or cooking oil
- ❑ salt and pepper
- ❑ shredded cheese

PREPARE AHEAD:

At home, crack open enough eggs to fill a sports bottle ¾ full. For each egg, add 1 tablespoon of milk. Put the cap on and shake **vigorously**. Keep in a cooler until you are ready to use.

DIRECTIONS:

1. Set camp stove to medium flame and heat up frying pan.
2. Add a pat of butter or a squirt of cooking oil to grease the pan.
3. Pour egg mixture into pan.
4. Add a dash of salt and pepper.
5. Sprinkle a handful of shredded cheese over the egg mixture.
6. As the mixture begins to bubble and clump together, flip and gently stir it with a spatula. Continue to do this until the mixture forms into large curds and no liquid is visible.

★ DOCTORED OATMEAL

Instant oatmeal is a quick and easy meal. Whole grains also keep you feeling full longer. You can buy packets of flavored oatmeal. But it's more fun to doctor up some plain oatmeal for your own breakfast creation.

INGREDIENTS:

❑ instant oatmeal (plain)
❑ water

OPTIONAL:
❑ fresh fruit (blueberries, strawberries, bananas, etc.)
❑ chocolate chips
❑ milk
❑ brown sugar, maple syrup, cinnamon
❑ granola

DIRECTIONS:

1. Boil a pot of water on the stove or fire.
2. Fill a mug or small bowl about half full of instant oatmeal.
3. Add boiling water until your mug or bowl is about ¾ full.
4. Stir and let sit for a couple minutes to cook and cool.
5. Top with your favorite optional ingredients, and then stir it up.

★ FLAPJACKS

Flapjacks—that's what you call pancakes while camping. They are one of the quickest and easiest (and most filling) breakfasts.

INGREDIENTS:

- ❑ instant pancake mix
- ❑ water
- ❑ butter
- ❑ maple syrup

OPTIONAL:

- ❑ fresh fruit
  (blueberries, strawberries, bananas, etc.)
- ❑ chocolate chips
- ❑ instant oatmeal or granola

PREPARE AHEAD:

Add 2 cups (250 grams) of pancake mix to a sports bottle. This should fill it about half full. Read the directions on the box to find out how much water you will need, but do not add water yet. Write the amount of water on a piece of tape and stick it to the bottle.

DIRECTIONS:

1. Add water to the sports bottle and shake, shake, shake it up!

2. Set camp stove to medium flame and heat up frying pan.

3. Use a pat of butter to grease the bottom of the pan.

4. Squeeze batter from the sports bottle into the pan. Don't make your pancakes too big, or they'll take longer to cook. It's best to make a couple small ones at a time.

5. Top with any of the optional ingredients.

6. When pancakes begin to bubble and the edges look dry, flip.

7. Cook pancakes until both sides are a dark golden brown.

8. Serve with butter and maple syrup.

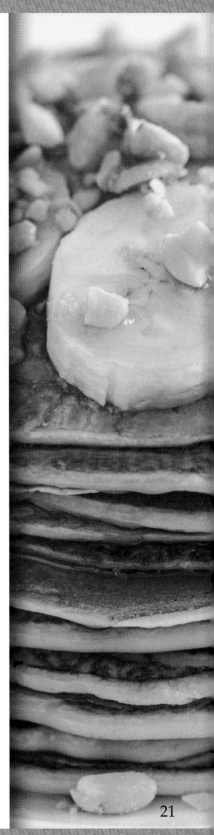

★ BREAKFAST HASH

One great thing about potatoes is that they are solid. Whether you're car camping or hiking in, spuds will not get squished when you pack them. Use them in many meals, such as breakfast hash.

INGREDIENTS:

- ❏ butter or cooking oil
- ❏ potatoes (medium size, any kind will work)
- ❏ salt and pepper
- ❏ chopped-up sausage or bacon
- ❏ cooked egg (optional)

OPTIONAL:

- ❏ onion powder
- ❏ garlic powder
- ❏ diced tomato or can of corn (drained)
- ❏ shredded cheese

PREPARE AHEAD:

If you're camping with a cooler, you can dice your potatoes and meat at home to save time later.

DIRECTIONS:

1. Set camp stove to medium flame and heat up frying pan.

2. Add a pat of butter or a squirt of oil to grease the pan.

3. Add 1 medium diced potato for each person eating (or fill pan half full).

4. Add a dash of salt and pepper. Add a dash of onion and garlic powder if desired.

5. Cook potatoes for 10 minutes, stir, and then cook for 10 minutes more.

6. Push the potatoes to one side of the frying pan and add sausage or bacon. Cook, stirring occasionally, until sausage is browned or the bacon is crispy.

7. Lower heat. Add tomatoes or corn and stir. Cook for 5 more minutes.

8. Turn off heat, sprinkle a handful of shredded cheese over potatoes, and serve.

9. Top with a cooked egg if desired.

CHAPTER 4

LUNCH AND SNACKS

It's easy to forget about lunch while out on your adventures. Don't do it! You need something to tide you over until dinner, whether it's an energy bar or homemade granola. Keeping your body fueled means you can keep having fun.

The recipes in this chapter are quick and easy. You can make them and go, with no cooking involved.

⭐ TORTILLA ROLL-UPS

Sandwiches are a quick and easy meal.
Make them more fun with tortillas!

INGREDIENTS:

- ❏ large flour tortillas
- ❏ sandwich meat
- ❏ sliced cheese

OPTIONAL:
- ❏ lettuce
- ❏ peanut butter and jelly
  (instead of meat and cheese)
- ❏ ketchup, mustard, or mayonnaise

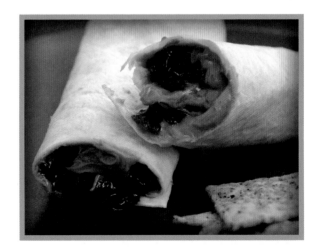

DIRECTIONS:

1. Take 1 tortilla and lay it flat.

2. Cover tortilla with 1 or 2 slices of sandwich meat.

3. Lay a slice of cheese on the meat.

4. Draw a line down the middle with your favorite condiment.

5. Take an edge of the tortilla farthest from the line of condiment and start rolling it up.

6. Put 1 or more roll-ups in a resealable bag for a quick sandwich you can eat on the go!

ROUGHING IT

Use flour tortillas instead of bread for sandwiches. Bread and buns can easily get squished, while tortillas are easy to pack.

★ SNACK STACKS

When you are on the trail, you may not want to stop for a long lunch. This simple snack will fill you up fast. Stack up different flavors for a tasty break!

INGREDIENTS:

- ❏ apples (1 per camper)
- ❏ cheese (block or sliced)
- ❏ summer sausage
- ❏ crackers

DIRECTIONS:

1. Cut apples into wedges.

2. Slice cheese into rectangles.

3. Cut sausage into thin wheels.

4. Make a stack: cracker, sausage wheel, cheese rectangle, and apple wedge.

5. Eat right away or pack in resealable bags for the trail.

 TRAIL MIX

Trail mix is one of the easiest take-it-with-you snacks. Ask your fellow campers about their favorite ingredients. Then make a big batch of trail mix before you leave. You can fill one bag for each camper to carry on the trail.

INGREDIENTS:

- ❏ nuts
  (peanuts, cashews almonds, etc.)
- ❏ dried fruit
  (raisins, bananas, cranberries, etc.)
- ❏ candy chips
  (chocolate, butterscotch, yogurt, etc.)

OPTIONAL:
- ❏ shelled sunflower seeds
- ❏ granola
- ❏ pretzels

MAKE AHEAD:

1. In a large bowl, combine nuts, dried fruit, and chocolate chips. (Use an equal amount of nuts and fruit and about half that amount of candy chips.)

2. Add optional ingredients.

3. Mix and store in resealable bags to snack on later.

CHAPTER 5
DINNER

As your day in the wild ends, your cooking fun is just beginning. Take time to prepare something special for dinner. You can also test your chef's skills by whipping up something over an open fire.

BUILDING A FIRE

A good cooking fire doesn't have roaring flames. You need coals to cook food evenly. When you start your cooking fire, add a few extra logs right away to get it roaring. When the flames start to die down, red-hot coals will start to form. With an adult's help, use a stick to spread the coals out in the firepit.

COOKING SAFETY

When cooking with fire, ask an adult to help out. Always keep a bucket of water or sand close to your cooking area. That way, if something catches fire, you can put it out fast.

⭐ PACKET MEALS

Packet dinners are simple, all-in-one meals. Each camper makes a packet, so every dinner is different.

INGREDIENTS:

- ❏ tinfoil
- ❏ hamburger (patties)
- ❏ potatoes
  (any kind will work;
   cut into small pieces)
- ❏ salt and pepper
- ❏ carrots (sliced into circles)

- ❏ diced onion
  (or onion powder)
- ❏ garlic powder

PREPARE AHEAD:

If you're camping with a cooler, you can slice carrots, dice onions, and make hamburger patties at home.

DIRECTIONS:

1. Take a square of tinfoil and spread it out flat.

2. Place hamburger patty in the middle of the foil.

3. Place 1 diced potato on top of burger.

4. Add a dash of salt and pepper (and garlic powder if desired).

5. Add some sliced carrots.

6. If desired, add diced onion or onion powder.

7. Wrap foil around everything.

8. Using tongs or oven glove, place packet in firepit on the outer edge.

9. Cook for 25 to 30 minutes.

★ PERSONAL PIZZAS

To make personal pizzas on an open fire, you will need a grate. On a stove, use a pan or grill.

INGREDIENTS:

- ❑ pita bread
- ❑ pizza or spaghetti sauce
- ❑ shredded cheese

OPTIONAL:
- ❑ pepperoni or cooked ground beef
- ❑ diced onion, tomato, and/or mushroom
- ❑ garlic powder and Italian seasoning

DIRECTIONS:

1. If using a grate or grill, cover surface with tinfoil before moving it over the fire.

2. Put pita bread on cooking surface, cook for about 30 seconds, and then flip, cooking for another 30 seconds.

3. Remove pita bread from grill.

4. Put 1 spoonful of sauce on pita bread and spread around. Add more sauce if needed.

5. Add any of the optional ingredients.

6. Lightly sprinkle cheese on top.

7. Place pita on cooking surface and heat until cheese begins to melt.

⭐ QUESADILLAS

If you want a quick and easy dinner (so that you can get to dessert sooner), quesadillas are the perfect choice. They are simple to make and filled with cheesy goodness.

INGREDIENTS:

❏ large tortillas
❏ shredded cheese

OPTIONAL:

❏ can of black beans, drained
❏ diced onion and tomato
❏ cooked chicken breast (shredded)
❏ salsa

DIRECTIONS:

1. Cover grilling surface with tinfoil.
2. Lay tortilla flat on a plate.
3. On one half of tortilla, sprinkle some cheese.
4. To the same half of the tortilla, add any of the optional ingredients.
5. Fold tortilla in half and then place on grill.
6. Cook until the bottom of the tortilla starts to brown and then flip.
7. Cook until both side of the tortilla are lightly brown and the cheese inside is melted.

COOKING SAFETY

If you use raw meat when cooking, be sure to know its safety temperature. Meats need to be heated to kill off harmful bacteria and germs. Eating undercooked meat can cause serious illness. Use these temperatures as a guide:

Beef .... 145 degrees Fahrenheit
(63 degrees Celsius)
Pork .... 145°F (63°C)
Seafood .... 145°F (63°C)
Ground meat .. 165°F (74°C)
Chicken .... 165°F (74°C)

CHAPTER 6

OVER-the-FIRE TREATS

No campout is complete without a campfire and a sweet treat. Almost everyone knows how to make s'mores or roast marshmallows over an open fire. Here are some other desserts that will impress your friends and family.

★ BANANA BOATS

S'mores are tasty, but banana boats deliver the gooey goodness of melted chocolate and marshmallows without all the mess.

INGREDIENTS:

- ❏ bananas
- ❏ chocolate chips
- ❏ marshmallows (minis work best)
- ❏ tinfoil

DIRECTIONS:

1. Make a slit lengthwise through a banana's peel, cutting about ¾ of the way into the banana. Be careful not to cut all the way through it.

2. Stuff the banana with chocolate chips and marshmallows.

3. Wrap the stuffed banana in tinfoil and set on the grate for about 5 minutes.

4. Remove from grate and let rest until cool enough to hold.

5. Grab a spoon and scoop the tasty goo into your mouth.

★ CAMPFIRE GRANOLA

Granola is a great trail treat. It doesn't melt or spoil, and you can add your favorite nuts and dried fruit for a healthy, energy-packed snack.

INGREDIENTS:

- ❑ nuts (pecans, cashews, or almonds)
- ❑ instant oatmeal
- ❑ cooking oil
- ❑ maple syrup
- ❑ dried fruit (cranberries, pineapple, etc.)

DIRECTIONS:

1. Warm cast-iron skillet over heat.

2. When pan is hot, add 2 cups (250 g) of nuts. Stir with a wooden spoon to keep them from burning.

3. When the nuts begin to brown and smell nutty, add 6 cups (480 g) of oatmeal. Continue to stir until the oatmeal begins to brown and get crispy.

4. Using an oven glove, remove skillet from heat. Add ¼ cup (60 milliliters) oil and ½ cup (120 mL) maple syrup and stir. Add more syrup as desired.

5. Add 1 cup (125 g) of dried fruit and mix.

6. Wait for granola to cool before munching.

★ CAMPFIRE PIES

A pie iron adds fun to campfire cooking. It makes pies, of course. It also makes grilled cheese sandwiches, tacos, and other goodies.

. . . .

INGREDIENTS:

❏ bread
❏ butter

FILLINGS:

❏ applesauce
❏ fruit pie filling
❏ jam

DIRECTIONS:

1. Butter 1 side of a piece of bread and set in pie iron with buttered side against the iron.

2. Press down in the middle of the bread to make a dent for the filling.

3. Add about 3 spoonfuls of filling.

4. Butter 1 side of a second piece of bread. Lay it on the filling with the butter side up.

5. Close the pie iron tightly and place over hot coals.

6. Cook for 3 minutes, and then flip and cook for another 3 minutes.

CHAPTER 7

LEAVE NO TRACE!

After the food is served and people are fed, you still have one important task. Clean up! Don't save it for tomorrow. Pack a small tub for washing dishes and some nature-friendly dish soap.

Dirty dishes will only become more difficult to scrub clean. Scraps of food will attract bugs and furry critters. And a sudden storm can scatter garbage all around the campground. Clean up before you relax.

CLEANING TIP

After cleaning up, don't just dump your dishwater in the woods. Save it to douse your fire before crawling into your sleeping bag.

TAKING TURNS

It's not fun to do *all* of the cooking or *all* of the cleaning. Create a chore chart to take turns. Let everyone pick a meal or meals to prepare. That will give them a chance to make one of their favorites. Those who are not cooking can take care of cleanup.

SHOW YOUR LOVE

As you enjoy the outdoors, remember to leave no trace of your visit! Whatever you bring into the wild, you should carry it back out. That will show your true love of nature and let other people enjoy it as well.

GET COOKING!

Whipping up meals in the wild can be a blast. If you plan ahead, your cooking adventures will be a success and you will have some tasty eats.

This book has set you on the right path. You know a few recipes and what gear you should pack. Test your recipes at home first. Practice using your camp stove or cooking over the coals. Get used to cooking with just a few tools. Soon you will be cooking like a pro—at home and in the wild!

BUILD A CHEF'S CAMPING SET

If you want to cook like a pro, you need the tools of a pro. Here is a list of items to help you with your cooking adventures. You may not need all of them, especially if you're roughing it. For a top-notch chef's camping set without gourmet prices, check out garage sales or ask adults for old cooking utensils that they no longer need.

- ☐ **knife**—a good chef's knife will be your most important tool
- ☐ **can opener**—one that also has a bottle opener
- ☐ **cutting board, small**
- ☐ **food thermometer**—to test the doneness of meat
- ☐ **headlamp**—so you can safely cook when it gets dark
- ☐ **measuring cup**
- ☐ **measuring spoons**
- ☐ **metal brush**—for cleaning the grate over a fire pit
- ☐ **oven gloves or tongs**—for when things get too hot to touch
- ☐ **roasting sticks**—for cooking marshmallows and hotdogs over the fire
- ☐ **spatula, metal**—for flipping burgers on a grill; it won't melt
- ☐ **spatula, plastic**—for flipping pancakes in a pan; it won't scratch the pan
- ☐ **wooden spoon or whisk**—for mixing and stirring

SPICING IT UP

To add some extra zest to your meals, don't forget the seasonings. Start with salt and pepper. A small dash of each will bring out the flavor in dishes from burgers to potatoes. Then add some basics or explore new flavors. Most spices can be bought in small containers. Or you can put spices from home in small, reusable shakers.

- ❏ garlic powder
- ❏ onion powder
- ❏ red pepper flakes
- ❏ salt and pepper

CONDIMENTS

Instead of toting big bottles of ketchup and mustard with you, consider small, squeezable bottles. They work well for cooking oil too. And if you're roughing it, they take up much less space. Don't forget to label them!

- ❏ cooking oil
- ❏ ketchup
- ❏ mayonnaise (keep cool)
- ❏ mustard

GLOSSARY

bacteria (bak-TIR-ee-ah)—microscopic organisms that live in soil, water, and the bodies of plants and animals; some can cause disease

canister (KAN-uh-stir)—small, round container

condiments (kuhn-DUH-mints)—things used to make food taste better

disposable (diss-POH-zuh-buhl)—something, such as a paper plate, that you throw away after using

edible (ED-uh-buhl)—safe to eat

forage (FOR-ij)—to search for food in the wild

grate (GRAYT)—a frame of metal bars used for cooking over a flame

propane (PROH-payn)—flammable gas used for fuel

reusable (ree-YOO-zuh-buhl)—something that can be used over and over again

roughing it (RUFF-ing it)—camping with very little gear

spoil (SPOIL)—in the case of food, to become rotten and inedible

toxic (TOK-sik)—having a harmful quality; toxic berries and leaves can cause extreme illnesses if eaten

utensils (yoo-TEN-suhl)—tools for eating, such as spoons, forks, and knives

vigorous (VIG-or-us)—done with force and energy

READ MORE

Bean, Raymond. *Backpacking Hacks: Camping Tips for Outdoor Adventures.* North Mankato, MN: Capstone, 2020.

Hamilton, David. *Family Foraging: A Fun Guide to Gathering and Eating Wild Plants.* Boulder, CO: Shambhala, 2019.

Morey, Allan. *Camping.* Mankato, MN: Amicus Ink, 2017.

INTERNET SITES

Active Kids—8 Campfire Recipes Kids Love to Make
https://www.activekids.com/parenting-and-family/articles/8-campfire-recipes-kids-love-to-make

Smokey Bear—How to Build Your Campfire
https://smokeybear.com/en/prevention-how-tos/campfire-safety/how-to-build-your-campfire

USDA—Food Safety Education for Kids and Teens
https://www.fsis.usda.gov/wps/portal/fsis/topics/food-safety-education/teach-others/download-materials/for-kids-and-teens

INDEX